IMAGES
of America

LONG BRANCH

IMAGES
of America

LONG BRANCH

[signature]

Paul Sniffen

ARCADIA

First published 1996
Copyright © Paul Sniffen, 1996

ISBN 0-7524-0298-6

Published by Arcadia Publishing,
an imprint of the Chalford Publishing Corporation
One Washington Center, Dover, New Hampshire 03820
Printed in Great Britain

Library of Congress Cataloging-in-Publication Data applied for

Contents

Dedication

This book is dedicated
to my great-great-grandmother,
Sarah Newlin Sniffen,
who started her photograph collection in the 1880s.

Introduction

Long Branch is a unique city with a history as interesting as it is long. Unfortunately, many aspects of this history have faded with the passage of time. For a while, stories of Long Branch's past were handed down from generation to generation, but with the migration of old families from the area, many of these stories have been lost. It is the intention of this photographic history of Long Branch to refresh some of those lost memories, and to rekindle interest in what is one of the greatest nineteenth-century American cities.

The coast of Long Branch was explored by John Cabot in 1498, Giovanni Da Verrazano in 1524, and Estevan Gomez in 1525. In 1664 Henry Hudson claimed the territory for the Netherlands, and it was originally settled by the Dutch. The area known as the Netherlands was later deeded to Charles II of England. James, Duke of York, eventually divided the land between the Hudson and Delaware into East and West Jersey and deeded the land to Lord Berkeley and Sir George Cateret. Berkeley and Cateret named it Nova Cesara.

Long Branch was settled by colonists who had migrated by way of Long Island seeking religious freedom. In 1665 Colonel Richard Nicholls allowed members of the Monmouth Patent to purchase land between Raritan Bay and the Atlantic Ocean. In 1668, John Slocum, Eliakim Wardell, Joseph Parker, Peter Parker, and a Mr. Hulet met with leaders of the Leni Lenape Indians to purchase land. There was a dispute between the Leni Lenape and the colonists over the amount of land to be purchased, but when the dispute was settled the boundaries of Long Branch were set. The name Long Branch came from the long branch of the Shrewsbury River on the north shore of the city.

In the eighteenth century Long Branch was inhabited by self-sufficient people who hunted, fished, and farmed, much as the Leni Lenape had done before them. In the nineteenth century, as shipping increased between New York and Philadelphia, the area began to expand rapidly. As the natural beauty of Long Branch became known, the rich and famous from New York, Philadelphia, and Washington, D.C., began to frequent the area. The waterfront soon evolved from an area of cottages and farmhouses to mansions and hotels, becoming the premier summer resort of the Northeast. Leaders in fashion, finance, theater, politics, and the military flocked to Long Branch by the hundreds. Among them were General Winfield Scott, Edwin Booth, Edwin Forrest, Maggie Mitchell, George W. Childs, George Pullman, Jim Fisk, Diamond Jim Brady, Lillian Russell, Horace Greeley, Lily Langtry, Henry Ward Beecher, "Buffalo" Bill Cody, General Phillip Sheridan, and General George Meade. As if this were not enough for the local economy, Presidents Chester A. Arthur, James A. Garfield, Ulysses S. Grant,

Rutherford B. Hayes, Benjamin Harrison, and William McKinley spent their summers at Long Branch, and President Woodrow Wilson stayed in West Long Branch.

In June 1881 President Garfield left Long Branch to return to Washington. On July 2 he was shot by Charles Jules Guiteau. The President returned to the Francklyn Cottage in Long Branch to recuperate from the gunshot wound, and a rail line was built from the Elberon station to the Francklyn Cottage to transport him. He never recovered, however, and died on September 19, 1881.

Today Long Branch is a bedroom community, with commuters using the New Jersey Transit buses and trains as well as the Garden State Parkway to travel north to work each day. Some family businesses that were started in the last century still exist in Long Branch, but many of the residents now work at the nearby Monmouth Medical Center, Fort Monmouth, and AT&T. Few people are aware of the area's historical and cultural importance. However, unlike many bedroom communities, Long Branch is now entering a period of renaissance. The beachfront is being redeveloped and Ocean Avenue is being expanded. Business and commerce on East and West Broadway and in West End are thriving, and many of the eighteenth-century homes are still lived in and maintained to high standards. Hopefully, this renewed interest in the area will cause people to investigate the history of Long Branch. Those that do have a great deal to discover. And those that live here, or were raised here, would no doubt agree with me: Long Branch is a great place to be from, as well as to return to.

One
Broadway

This 1907 photograph shows the section of Broadway between Liberty Street and Third Avenue. Among the businesses that called Broadway home at this time were J. Hicks, jeweler, at 180 Broadway, and Joseph Goldstein's department store, which can be seen in the right-hand corner of this photograph. This image testifies to the fact that in the first decade of the twentieth century city streets still saw far more horses than automobiles. (Durnell Collection.)

This 1907 scene on Broadway shows Steinbach's department store on the left and Liberman's shoe store and Leowitz's paint store on the right. Note the motorcycle and the bicycles at the curbs. (Durnell Collection.)

This view shows Broadway, looking toward Liberty Street, in 1888. The snowstorm may be the famous "Blizzard of '88" that newspapers reported as stopping all forms of transportation for days. What appears to be a trolley track in the foreground is really a curb or sidewalk with sled tracks alongside it. (Durnell Collection.)

The top half of this 1909 image shows the north side of Broadway as seen from Liberty Street, in a photograph taken by Cottrell; the bottom half shows Liberty Street as seen from Broadway, in an photograph from the Jacob Gassman & Son photography shop. (Durnell Collection.)

This 1909 image shows the south side of Broadway looking east (top) and the Broadway Bus Company (bottom). Maggie Mitchell's cottage is located behind the buses in the bottom section. (Durnell Collection.)

This photograph of the north side of Broadway west of Norwood Avenue was taken in 1995 to show some the original architectural elements that remain on the street. Note that the building in the center still has its nineteenth-century rooftop, windows, and storefront design. (Sniffen Collection.)

The north side of Broadway is shown here in a view looking east toward St. Luke's Methodist Church. The storefront and the top of the white building still retain their nineteenth-century appearance. (Sniffen Collection.)

This is the north side of Broadway looking west. (Sniffen Collection.)

The bank in this view of the north side of Broadway looking west was organized in 1872. The building is now occupied by Nat West Bank. (Sniffen Collection.)

This view of Broadway shows that many buildings retain their original appearance on the second floor and above, while the storefronts have been remodeled, probably many times as styles have changed over the years. (Sniffen Collection.)

The north side of Broadway is shown here, looking east. Only the bricked upper windows of the tall white building give us a clue that this section of town was developed in the Victorian era. (Sniffen Collection.)

Despite today's laudable preservation efforts, many buildings have still been rebuilt or remodeled to serve new purposes, as they have been since time immemorial. So much is lost, though, and it is often not until years later that we appreciate quite how much. This photograph shows that in this section of Broadway only the building in the center retains its nineteenth-century architecture. (Sniffen Collection.)

This section of Broadway, however, has many buildings lucky enough to retain their original style. (Sniffen Collection.)

This view is of the south side of Broadway looking east. (Sniffen Collection.)

Brighton Avenue in West End is shown here in a view looking east. (Sniffen Collection.)

The Long Branch Free Public Library is located on Broadway. (Sniffen Collection.)

This group of buildings is opposite the library. Nineteenth-century architecture is still prominent on Broadway. (Sniffen Collection.)

The Old Masonic Temple on Broadway is now the Long Branch Covenant Church. (Sniffen Collection.)

The old Long Branch City Hall on Broadway, complete with bell tower and clock, is shown here. (Durnell Collection.)

Looking east on Broadway in 1908, Steinbach's department store is on the left. Steinbach's now has locations in Red Bank and Neptune. (Durnell Collection.)

Note the abundance of poles and wires in this view looking west on Broadway in the mid-1800s. At this time they would have supplied electricity to some homes and businesses and carried telegraph or telephone cables. The horse-drawn wagon on the right is illegally parked in front of a fire hydrant, which may be next to a fire station on the right. (Durnell Collection.)

This image dates from July 1870, and advises: "No children, you had better wear tunics. You see a full figure looks well in any suit. Now if you only had a figure you could capture millionaires in any costume." (Durnell Collection.)

Some of Broadway's nineteenth-century buildings were in various states of renovation when this image was taken in 1995. Photography of this nature is tremendously useful for the historic record: the patchy archives that we as a society possess of the nineteenth century and even the twentieth should teach us that even ordinary scenes are worth preserving on film for future generations to learn from. (Sniffen Collection.)

Two
Business and Commerce

This 1883 view of 508 Broadway shows the Long Branch Post Office and the law offices of W.S.B. Parker and Wilbur A. Heisley. (Durnell Collection.)

Cheers Food & Drink is located in a nineteenth-century building across the street from city hall. (Sniffen Collection.)

Nineteenth-century storefronts on the north side of Brighton Avenue are shown here as they looked more than a century after they were built. (Sniffen Collection.)

24

Brighton Avenue is shown here in a view looking east toward the ocean. (Sniffen Collection.)

This is the south side of Broadway, in another view looking east toward the ocean. (Sniffen Collection.)

This photograph of P. Troutman's drugstore was taken by local photographer Gustav Pach in 1881. Note the boardwalk in front of the stores. (Durnell Collection.)

Broadway has always been the business center of Long Branch. This 1875 photograph shows the Morford & Vanderveer Hardware Store, at 510–512 Broadway (west of Norwood Avenue). Morford and Vanderveer established the business in 1835 and moved to this site in 1875. H.B. Sherman's feed store can be seen on the left. (Durnell Collection.)

This 1880 photograph, taken by Gustav Pach, shows his photography gallery. The gallery was located on the grounds of the United States Hotel. Until the camera became inexpensive enough to become a household possession, galleries like this one were an important service in every town, and were probably visited by all but the poorest residents on special occasions of one sort or another. The Pach family had studios and galleries all over New York and New Jersey that were in operation from 1867 until the 1980s. (Durnell Collection.)

The printing office of Jas. B. Morris' *Long Branch News* was photographed in 1876. This paper was succeeded by the *Long Branch Record*, which continued publishing until the 1980s. (Durnell Collection.)

Members of the Long Branch Chamber of Commerce are shown here in 1916. These town fathers would be sending their sons to war in Europe just one year later. (Durnell Collection.)

This 1995 photograph of the north side of Brighton Avenue shows nineteenth-century architecture at the top of the buildings and twentieth-century designs at the bottom on the storefronts. (Sniffen Collection.)

Three

Fire Department

Oliver Byron Engine Company No. 5 was located near Ocean Avenue in North Long Branch. The company was a member of IOOF, which I believe was the International Order of Firefighters. During the nineteenth century, most towns and cities did not have municipal firefighting crews, but rather were protected by private firefighting and insurance companies or by volunteer crews. The sign at the lower right advertises that the Seaview Lodge meets at the fire station on Monday nights. The building to the left is no longer in existence. (Durnell Collection.)

This nineteenth-century horse-drawn pumper was photographed in front of one of Long Branch's nine fire stations. It is not clear whether this is a hand or steam pumper, but we know that it is a four-horsepower wagon. Nineteenth-century townspeople were great celebraters and paraders: many of the photographs from this time show the town decorated for a variety of special events and celebrations. In the days when our world was a much smaller one, and in the days before the television, people entertained themselves with social events. It is unclear what the occasion was when this photograph was taken, but a effort had certainly been made to decorate every building in town. (Durnell Collection.)

Phil Daly Hose Company No. 2 was still using this reliable horse-drawn pumper in 1912. Fred Taber is driving, with Harry P. Heldt and Harold Adamson in the center and Father Halloran and Ed Miller at the rear. (Durnell Collection.)

Oliver D. Byron (1842–1920) acting in the play *The Plunger* in 1880. Oliver Byron Engine Company No. 5 was named after him. (Durnell Collection.)

Oliver Byron Engine Company No. 5 on Atlantic Avenue is shown here in 1995. (Sniffen Collection.)

Long Branch Fire Station 25-2 on Branchport Avenue is also known as Branchport Hose Company No. 3. (Sniffen Collection.)

Neptune Hose Company No. 1 was organized in 1877 and located at 30 Branchport Avenue. It is now Long Branch Fire Station 25-5. This photograph was taken in 1995 (Sniffen Collection.)

Oceanic Truck and Engine Company No. 1 is located at the intersection of Norwood Avenue and Broadway. (Sniffen Collection.)

West End Engine Company No. 3 is located at the intersection of Second Avenue and Montgomery Street in West End. (Sniffen Collection.)

Atlantic Engine Company No. 2 is located on Broadway, across the street from the library and city hall. (Sniffen Collection.)

Elberon Engine Company No. 4 was established in 1890 and located across the street from the Elberon station and the library. (Sniffen Collection.)

This satire appeared in *Life Magazine* in July 1883. The man in the top hat is carrying a bag labeled "City Boarder to Long Branch." (Durnell Collection.)

Independent Engine and Truck Company No. 2 and Phil Daly Hose Company No. 2 are located off the north side of Broadway. (Sniffen Collection.)

Four
Actors and Actresses

Mrs. D.P. Bowers stayed at the West End Hotel in 1888. Here she portrays one of the queens of Europe, probably in a Shakespeare play. (Durnell Collection.)

Actress Louise Montague spent her summers at Hollywood, Long Branch. This photograph was taken in 1890, possibly for promotional purposes. (Durnell Collection.)

Lillian Russell, "the first pin up girl," is shown here in an 1879 photograph. (Durnell Collection.)

Lenore Ulrich, who starred in *The Heart of Wetona*, stayed at the Hollywood Hotel in West End in 1916. (Durnell Collection.)

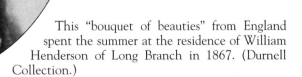

This "bouquet of beauties" from England spent the summer at the residence of William Henderson of Long Branch in 1867. (Durnell Collection.)

Maude Adams (1872–1953) appeared in *L'aiglon* in 1901. (Durnell Collection.)

Actress Vernona Jerbeau (1861–1914) spent her summers at Long Branch. This photographic portrait was made in 1885. (Durnell Collection.)

Della spent her summers in North Long Branch in the 1890s. (Durnell Collection.)

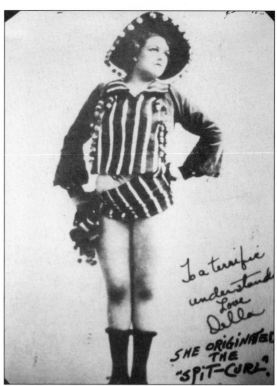

Annie Russell (1864–1936) stayed at the Hollywood Hotel while she was acting in *Mice and Men* in 1903. (Durnell Collection.)

Elsie Ferguson (1885–1961) was an actress and a summer visitor to Long Branch. (Durnell Collection.)

Miss Williams and Richard Carle opened the Broadway Theater in Long Branch in 1912. They spent their summers in Carle's cottage on Myrtle Avenue. (Durnell Collection.)

William R. Floyd (1835–1880) was both an actor and a stage manager for Lester Wallack. This photograph was taken in 1870. (Durnell Collection.)

These are a few of the many dozens of actors and actresses that performed in Long Branch from May to September each year. (Durnell Collection.)

These are still more of the many actors and actresses that performed for the rich and famous during the summer at Long Branch. (Durnell Collection.)

This is the cast of the production of *The Merry Widow* that was staged at Pleasure Bay in 1907. (Durnell Collection.)

Five

North Long Branch

These nineteenth-century storefronts are located on the south side of Atlantic Avenue in North Long Branch. (Sniffen Collection.)

This photograph of nineteenth-century storefronts on the south side of Atlantic Avenue in North Long Branch was taken in 1995. (Sniffen Collection.)

These nineteenth-century buildings on the north side of Atlantic Avenue in North Long Branch were photographed in 1995. (Sniffen Collection.)

Price's Dock at Pleasure Bay, North Long Branch, is shown here in 1905. (Durnell Collection.)

This view of the Pleasure Bay Casino and the North Long Branch trolley terminal was taken by local photographer Falk in 1895. (Durnell Collection.)

The Bridgeport Inn is shown here on the left with the bridge in the background. The inn was located in the area now known as Branchport in the northwest part of Long Branch. (Durnell Collection.)

It is not clear if this photograph, taken in 1898 on Pleasure Bay, is of a real naval vessel or of a large prop to be used in a performance of the play *H.M.S. Pinafore*. (Durnell Collection.)

Six
The Oceanfront

The *Plymouth Rock* was photographed landing at the Long Branch Pier in 1880. The Long Branch Pier was one of the few piers in the world that could accommodate ocean-going vessels. This three-deck steamboat carried hundreds of passengers up and down the Jersey Coast during the late nineteenth and early twentieth centuries. (Durnell Collection.)

This postcard view of a beautiful summer day along the Boardwalk was sent to Miss Eva Miller in Sacramento, California.

ON THE BEACH. LONG BRANCH.

"Greetings from Picturesque America." This postcard was published by Arthur Livingstone in New York and sent in 1904 to Miss Stella E. Jones.

The pier is barely visible to the right in this view looking north on Ocean Avenue on a foggy day. The sidewalk and road appear to be dirt or gravel. (Durnell Collection.)

This is a view from the old iron pier looking north from Broadway in 1900. Note the roped swimming area in the background. (Durnell Collection.)

Note that sidewalks and curbs are present in this view looking north on Ocean Avenue from Bath Avenue in 1908, but the roadway still consists of dirt. (Durnell Collection.)

This photograph was taken looking south on Ocean Avenue from Bath Avenue in 1915. (Durnell Collection.)

This interesting photograph shows the view looking south from the iron pier as it would have looked to a visitor in 1900. The Mansion House can be seen on the right and the United States Hotel is just visible in the distance. (Durnell Collection.)

This photograph, taken looking north at Chelsea Avenue, shows Cranmer's Pavilion at Bluff Walk and Drive as it appeared in 1907. Note the combination of automobiles and horses on the dirt surface of Ocean Avenue. (Durnell Collection.)

In this 1906 scene in front of Ocean Hotel, the boardwalk and pier can be seen to the right. (Durnell Collection.)

This 1995 photograph, taken looking north from the boardwalk, offers an interesting contrast to the previous image. Unfortunately, the pier has not been in use for several years as a result of a fire and storm damage. (Sniffen Collection.)

Looking south from the boardwalk, this photograph was also taken in 1995. (Sniffen Collection.)

The Hilton Hotel is on the left in this view looking north on the pier and boardwalk in 1995. (Sniffen Collection.)

This postcard of the Cassino annex and bandstand was sent to Mrs. A. Muller. It was postmarked August 29, 1907.

A telegraphers' meeting was held at Long Branch on September 12, 1895. Groups would often gather for a "day out" at seaside resorts like Long Branch in the nineteenth and early twentieth centuries. This photograph was taken at the boardwalk. Note the pier and the ship in the background. (Durnell Collection.)

The Casino on Ocean Avenue is shown here in the early 1900s. (Durnell Collection.)

The "New Scenic Railway" was photographed around the turn of the century. Today such rides are known as roller coasters. This structure is long gone. (Durnell Collection.)

Sadly, this twentieth-century roller coaster at the beach no longer exists. (Durnell Collection.)

This photograph of a hot summer day around the turn of the century proves that, at that time, sun screen was obviously not a necessity. (Durnell Collection.)

The Stella Maris Retreat was located on Ocean Avenue in Elberon. (Sniffen Collection.)

Seven Presidents Park is located on Ocean Avenue at the beach. (Sniffen Collection.)

Seven
Presidents and
Generals

This statue of James Abram Garfield, the twentieth president of the United States, was dedicated on September 2, 1918. Born in Mentor, Ohio, on November 19, 1831, Garfield died at Long Branch. His statue is now located between the Hilton Hotel and the Atlantic Ocean. (Durnell Collection.)

President William McKinley spent his summers at Long Branch. It was actually easier to make the trip to and from Washington by train around the turn of the century than it is today.

General Phillip Sheridan was a frequent visitor to Long Branch as well as a good friend of "Buffalo" Bill Cody. (Durnell Collection.)

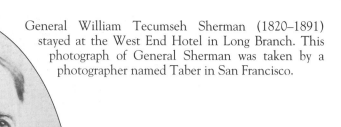

General William Tecumseh Sherman (1820–1891) stayed at the West End Hotel in Long Branch. This photograph of General Sherman was taken by a photographer named Taber in San Francisco.

President and Mrs. Rutherford B. Hayes posed for an 1877 photograph by local photographer Pach.

General Phillip Sheridan (1831–1888) had this photograph taken during a 1865 stay at the West End Hotel. (Durnell Collection.)

General Ulysses S. Grant is shown here at George W. Childs' cottage in an 1870 photograph taken by Pach. Mr. Childs is standing on the right. (Durnell Collection.)

This photograph of President Ulysses S. Grant was taken three days before his death on July 20, 1895. (Durnell Collection.)

President Abraham Lincoln never came to Long Branch while in office, but he did visit several years earlier when he was a member of congress. (Durnell Collection.)

Eight

Transportation

This group is waiting for the 6 pm train at the old Long Branch railroad station. The wagons on the left are probably horse-drawn livery cabs. The trains on the tracks on the right are probably out of service. (Durnell Collection.)

These trotters were photographed in action at the track in Hollywood in 1909. Hollywood is now known as West End. Trotters and pacers now race in Freehold. (Durnell Collection.)

Alfred G. Vanderbilt's horses-drawn carriage bolts down Ocean Avenue during the 1905 race from Sea Bright to Hollywood. They covered the 6 miles of the course in twenty-six minutes, or at about 40 miles per hour. It is interesting to note that it takes the same time to travel this route by car today! (Durnell Collection.)

This steeplechase occurred at the Society Circus in Hollwood in 1909. This event now takes place at Monmouth Park in Oceanport. (Durnell Collection.)

All types of equestrian events took place at the Hollywood Track in West End in 1909. (Durnell Collection.)

It was obviously a warm day when this Long Branch Bus Company coach was photographed in 1920 because all of the windows are open. Note the roller on the left for leveling the road surface. (Durnell Collection.)

This was the first horse show at the Hollywood Track in West End. (Durnell Collection.)

Transportation evolved quite quickly from horse-drawn wagons, to horse-drawn trolleys, and then to electric trolleys before 1900. The development of the electric trolley in particular revolutionized public transportation. As trolley networks spread over even rural areas of the United States, people became much more mobile. The electric trolley car was also a critical factor in the development of seaside resorts along the coast of New Jersey, as visitors from the cities could easily take a trolley to the coast for the day. (Durnell Collection.)

A steam locomotive makes a stop at Long Branch in the mid-nineteenth century. (Durnell Collection.)

The Long Branch railroad depot is shown here in the mid-nineteenth century. (Durnell Collection.)

President Garfield was taken here, the Elberon train station, after he suffered a gunshot wound in a Washington railroad station on July 2, 1881. He died in Elberon on September 19, 1881. The original station burned down a few years ago. (Sniffen Collection.)

According to the August 1872 edition of the London newspaper *Days Doings*, this was "the surprise party that waited on an inquisitive young man from Connecticut." (Durnell Collection.)

This horse and carriage race at the Hollywood Track in West End was photographed in 1909. (Durnell Collection.)

Nine
Hotels and Cottages

This 1942 photograph shows the Phil Daly mansion at the corner of Chelsea and Second Avenues. Phil had two of these so-called "cottages" built in 1886. He rented one to Lily Langtry and Senator James Smith Jr. (Durnell Collection.)

This interesting nineteenth-century home was located on Chelsea Avenue. (Sniffen Collection.)

This typical nineteenth-century home, complete with a porch for relaxing during the summer, was located on Woodgate Avenue along the shore. (Sniffen Collection.)

Long Branch is blessed with many well-preserved Victorian homes. The porch on this home, located on Atlantic Avenue, allowed residents to catch the sun, shade, or breeze from any direction. Multiple chimneys for fireplaces were common at this time. (Sniffen Collection.)

R. Horace Curtis's cottage was located on Grand Avenue at the turn of the century. (Durnell Collection.)

This photograph of a beautiful Long Branch mansion was taken in 1882. Note the brick foundation, two chimneys, and the breezeway allowing horses and carriages to pass through. (Durnell Collection.)

Clarence J. Housman's home on Hollywood Avenue in West End was designed by architect Harry Allan Jacobs. Housman was the mayor of Long Branch from 1920 to 1924. This photograph is dated 1911. (Durnell Collection.)

This is a 1905 view of Alfred J. Nathan's cottage in Elberon. The cottage was designed by architect A.J. Manning and built in 1902. (Durnell Collection.)

This 1885 photograph shows a cottage built by Mr. Newcomb, who was a banker, railroad executive, and a close friend of President Grant. The building was sold in 1911 to Lyman Bloomingdale of the famous department store. (Durnell Collection.)

Lewis B. Brown's cottage at the corner of Ocean and Sycamore Avenues in Elberon was photographed by Pach in 1877. Mr. Brown, a founder of Elberon, died here in 1900. Daniel Guggenheim built his villa, "Firenzie," on this site in 1903. (Durnell Collection.)

"Firenzie" was designed by architects Carrere & Hastings. The villa burned in 1941. (Durnell Collection.)

This 1907 photograph shows Henry Seligman's villa, "Shorelands," on Ocean Avenue in Elberon. It was designed by architect C.P.H. Gilbert and built in 1902. (Durnell Collection.)

"Firenzie" is shown here in 1909. The villa was purchased by Helen V. Stern in 1940, just one year before it was destroyed by fire. (Durnell Collection.)

This photograph shows the Florence Hotel on Ocean Avenue in Long Branch. Note that in this era hotel owners and visitors alike were not particularly concerned about how they might exit the building in case of fire, as there are no fire escapes at all. (Durnell Collection.)

"Ocean Crest" was owned by George H. Curtis, son of Jerimiah Curtis, and located at 747 Ocean Avenue. (Durnell Collection.)

Pach took this photograph of Oliver D. Byron's cottage at Ocean and Atlantic Avenues in 1868. This cottage still stands today. It is located one block away from the fire station that is named after Byron. (Durnell Collection.)

President Grant's cottage is shown here in 1907. It was later owned by Miss A.L. Price (1877–1947) and her husband, Harry B. Goldsmith. (Durnell Collection.)

The Charles D. Cook cottage on Lincoln Avenue in Elberon was photographed in 1885. This summer home was designed by architects McKim, Mead & White and cost $30,000 to build. Mr. Cook was the president of Tiffany & Co. of New York. (Durnell Collection.)

This nineteenth-century home on Second Avenue in Long Branch features a wrap-around porch. Such porches were often closed in by twentieth-century owners to provide more living space. (Sniffen Collection.)

The exterior of the original home of Frank M. McDermit, located on Woodgate Avenue, has survived almost unchanged since 1915. (Sniffen Collection.)

This photograph of the home of Frank M. McDermit was taken in 1915. Unlike many streets at this time, Woodgate Avenue was paved and had sidewalks and curbs. (Durnell Collection.)

Pach photographed this seaside cottage in 1885. Among the residents and guests that stayed here was a certain James Seligman, who visited in 1873. James and his brother William came to the United States from Bavaria in 1839 to join their brother Joseph, who arrived in 1833. (Durnell Collection.)

This cottage was built by Mr. N.W. Chater in 1865. In 1873 Chater sold the cottage to Mortimer Hendricks. In 1904 the cottage was the summer home of Leonard Lewisohn. This photograph of the cottage was taken by Pach in 1868. (Durnell Collection.)

The original owner of this seashore cottage is unknown. Like many oceanfront homes, the cottage had shutters to protect it against the damage caused by storms blowing off the Atlantic. (Durnell Collection.)

The original owner of "The Avery" was R.J. Dobbins. The cottage was located at the southwest corner of the Matilda Terrace and Ocean Avenue intersection. (Durnell Collection.)

William F. Leach's cottage on Ocean Avenue (opposite Sternberger Avenue) was photographed by Pach in 1869. In 1896 Samuel Untermeyer rented the cottage and in 1905 it was occupied by David Heller. (Durnell Collection.)

This is an 1897 view of Phil Daly's Pennsylvania Club. Built in 1860 by John F. Chamberlin, the club was located on the southwest corner of the Ocean and Brighton Avenue intersection. (Durnell Collection.)

"Ocean Lawn," at 755 Ocean Avenue, was originally owned by Jeremiah W. Curtis. (Durnell Collection.)

This is an 1896 view of the Thomas G. Patten residence at Pleasure Bay on the Shrewsbury River. The building is now home to the Patten Point Yacht Club. (Durnell Collection.)

This cottage, built in 1883, is located on the northeast corner of the Lincoln and Elberon Avenue intersection in Elberon. (Durnell Collection.)

The Henry T. Helmbold cottage was built in 1866. Perhaps Helmbold commissioned Pach to take this photograph in 1882 to record the special event that he was hosting. (Durnell Collection.)

Phil Daly's Pennsylvania Club entertained the rich and famous for many years. This photograph was taken in 1901. (Durnell Collection.)

This classic nineteenth-century home is located on Cedar Avenue in Long Branch. Note the symetrical design. (Sniffen Collection.)

The Dr. William Rockwell cottage is shown here in 1867. (Durnell Collection.)

This image of life at the Continental Hotel was created in 1871. This hotel was a favorite of Jim Fisk, Jay Gould, and many other notables. In 1873 it became Deland's Ocean Hotel. (Durnell Collection.)

Ten
Churches and Schools

The "Our Lady Star of the Sea" Church is located on the corner of Chelsea and Second Avenues. (Sniffen Collection.)

This is an 1885 view of the "Our Lady Star of the Sea" Church on the northeast corner of the Chelsea and Second Avenue intersection. When the church was built in 1876, the pastor was Father John Salann. The church burned down in 1926. (Durnell Collection.)

The Asbury Methodist Church on Atlantic Avenue in North Long Branch was founded in 1869. (Sniffen Collection.)

The Asbury Methodist Church on the north side of Atlantic Avenue celebrated its 125th anniversary in 1994. (Sniffen Collection.)

The Long Branch Public School Annex on the northeast corner of the Third and Chelsea Avenue intersection was built in 1906 as a parochial school. (Sniffen Collection.)

The parochial school on the northeast corner of Third and Chelsea Avenues was built in 1906. Today it is the Long Branch Public School Annex. (Durnell Collection.)

This is Primary School No. 3 on Church Street in North Long Branch. (Sniffen Collection.)

The Chattle High School and Grammar School on Morris Avenue is shown here in 1906. (Durnell Collection.)

The Church of the Seven Presidents is located on Ocean Avenue in Elberon. Presidents Garfield, Grant, Harrison, Hayes, McKinley, and Wilson have all attended services here. Today it is the home of the Long Branch Historical Society. (Sniffen Collection.)

St. Michaels Roman Catholic Church is located on Ocean Avenue, near Takanansee Lake. (Sniffen Collection.)

The Baptist church is located on Chelsea Avenue, on land that was formerly the property of Peter Hand. (Sniffen Collection.)

These were some of the teachers and officers at the Methodist Church Sunday School Centenary. The two Methodist churches in Long Branch are St. Luke's Methodist Church and the Asbury Methodist Church. (Durnell Collection.)

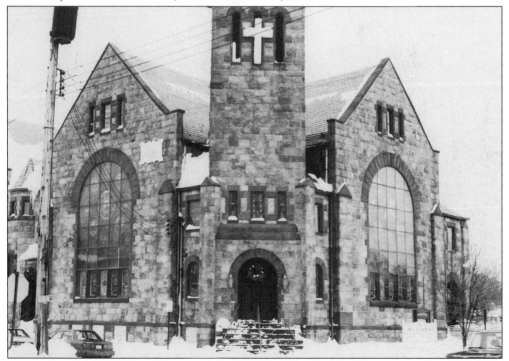

St. Luke's Methodist Church is located on Broadway. (Sniffen Collection.)

St. Stephanos Church is located on Ocean Avenue in Elberon. (Sniffen Collection.)

This is the old Second Baptist Church, located on Liberty Street in Long Branch. (Sniffen Collection.)

Eleven
Monmouth Memorial

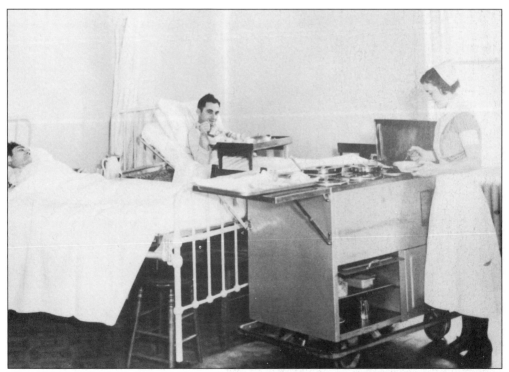

This photograph was taken during meal time at Monmouth Memorial Hospital in the early 1900s. (Monmouth Medical Center Collection.)

The Mary Owen Borden Pavilion (on the left) was added to Monmouth Memorial Hospital in 1940 and the Community Wing (on the right) was added in 1950. (Sniffen Collection.)

The E. Murray Todd Building was added to Monmouth Medical Center in 1987. (Sniffen Collection.)

The Robert C. Stanley Wing was added to Monmouth Medical Center in 1979. (Monmouth Medical Center Collection.)

Arnold's Delicatessen on Broadway is allegedly where the first doctors and laymen met to discuss the establishment of a hospital in this area. (Monmouth Medical Center Collection.)

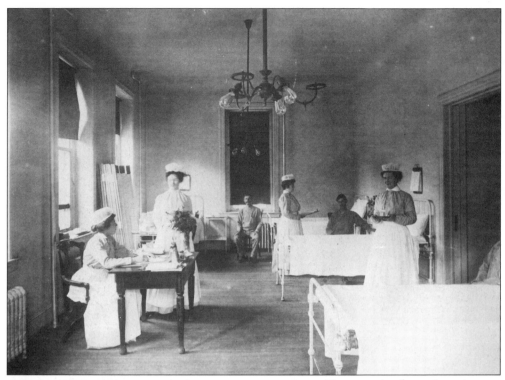

Nurses caring for patients in a ward of Monmouth Memorial Hospital were photographed around the turn of the century. Note the electric lamps on the ceiling. (Monmouth Medical Center Collection.)

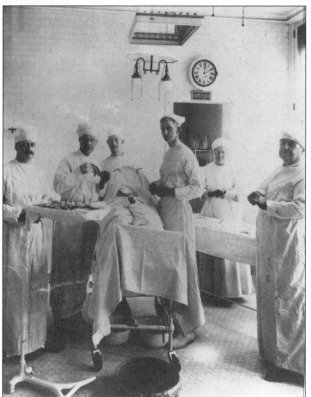

This surgery looks almost barbaric to the modern eye, but when this turn-of-the-century photograph was taken, the methods and approach were actually totally up-to-date. The sign under the clock reads "Silence." Electric lamps can be seen to the left of the clock. (Monmouth Medical Center Collection.)

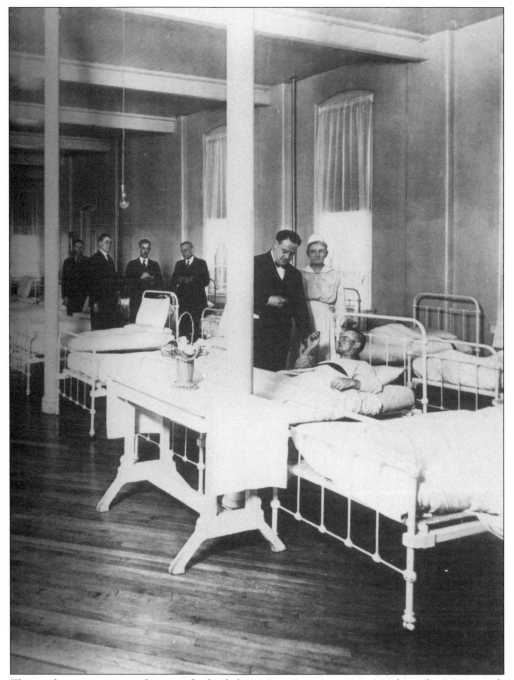

These physicians were photographed while visiting patients in a ward at the Monmouth Memorial Hospital. The hospital was originally housed in a building that first saw use as the Central Hotel. (Monmouth Medical Center Collection.)

The Mammouth Circus performed in Sea Bright to benefit Monmouth Memorial Hospital. This photograph was taken by Pach. (Monmouth Medical Center Collection.)

This Monmouth Memorial Hospital graduate nurse was photographed in 1940 for the *Monmouth Pictorial*, the hospital's quarterly newsletter. (Monmouth Medical Center Collection.)

Dr. Edwin Field and several nurses were photographed with Bud Hartsgrove, an appendectomy patient, around the turn of the century. (Monmouth Medical Center Collection.)

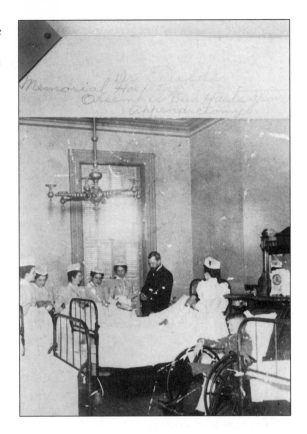

The Monmouth Memorial Hospital Nursing School was founded in 1896. Happy anniversary to the members of a profession that is often not appreciated as much as it should be! (Monmouth Medical Center Collection.)

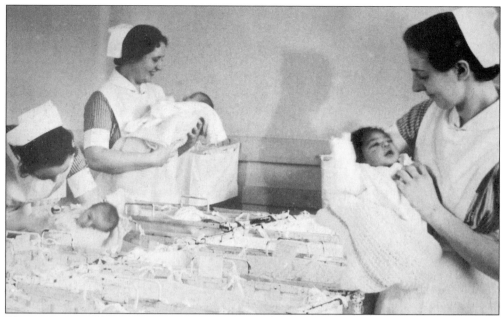

The nursery at the Monmouth Memorial Hospital is shown here in the early 1900s. (Monmouth Medical Center Collection.)

These nursing cadets at Monmouth Memorial Hospital were photographed during World War II. (Monmouth Medical Center Collection.)

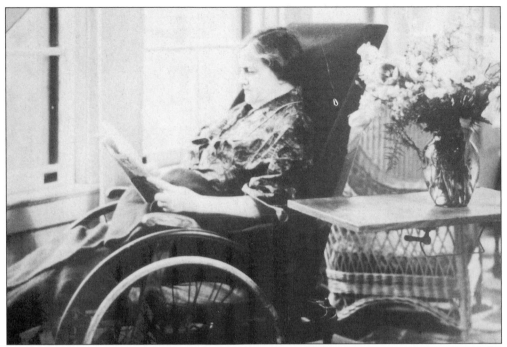

This patient was photographed at Monmouth Memorial Hospital in the early years of the twentieth century. (Monmouth Medical Center Collection.)

The Class of 1936 at the Monmouth Memorial Hospital Nursing School posed for this class picture. (Monmouth Medical Center Collection.)

These Monmouth Memorial Hospital Nursing School graduates are shown here in the early 1900s. (Monmouth Medical Center Collection.)

Most nurses lived on-site while they completed their training. This *c.* 1910 photograph shows a nurses' residence at Monmouth Memorial Hospital. (Monmouth Medical Center Collection.)

1904

These beautiful young women were graduates of the Monmouth Memorial Hospital Nursing School in 1904. (Monmouth Medical Center Collection.)

This satire about Long Branch appeared in the August 1871 edition of London's *Days Doings*.

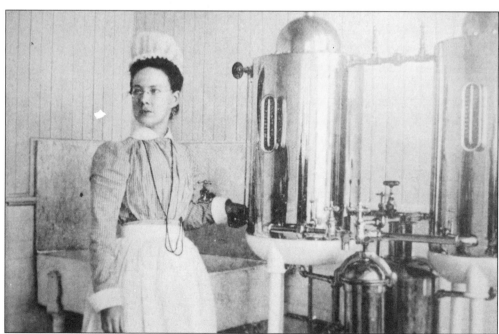

This nurse was photographed while operating sterilizing equipment at Monmouth Memorial Hospital around the turn of the century. (Monmouth Medical Center Collection.)

Twelve
Ladies and Gentlemen

Mrs. Abraham Lincoln spent the summer at the Mansion House in 1861. President Lincoln never came to Long Branch while he was president, but he did visit earlier when he was a member of congress. (Durnell Collection.)

Mrs. Frank Quinn (on the right) was a faithful and untiring worker at St. James Church in Long Branch. The ladies to her left are unidentified. (Durnell Collection.)

Mrs. Chanfrau lived on Cedar Avenue in Long Branch in the mid-nineteenth century. (Durnell Collection.)

Sarah Newlin Sniffen visited Long Branch on many occassions and began collecting photographs of Long Branch in the 1880s. (Sniffen Collection.)

Margaret "Maggie" Mitchell was photographed in 1865 by Matthew Brady, the famous Civil War photographer. (Durnell Collection.)

Thomas Gedney Patten and Walter Renwick Patten founded the Patten Steamship Line at Pleasure Bay. Thomas Patten also served at various times as a New York congressman and as postmaster for New York City. (Durnell Collection.)

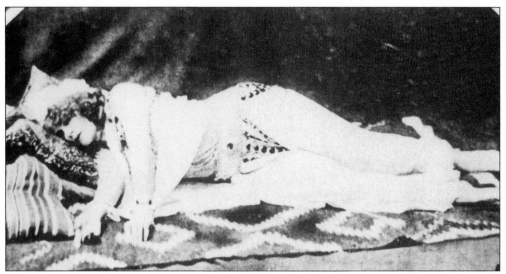

A West End Hotel guest in 1906. (Durnell Collection.)

Frank S. Chanfrau (1824–1884) lived on Cedar Avenue when this photograph was taken by Pach in 1870. (Durnell Collection.)

Edwin Forrest (1806–1872) lived and
worked in Long Branch for many years.
(Durnell Collection.)

Colonel James Fisk Jr. spent his
summers at the Continental Hotel.
This photograph was taken in 1870
aboard the ship the *Plymouth Rock*.
(Durnell Collection.)

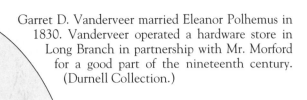

Garret D. Vanderveer married Eleanor Polhemus in 1830. Vanderveer operated a hardware store in Long Branch in partnership with Mr. Morford for a good part of the nineteenth century. (Durnell Collection.)

Lewis Blanchard Brown (1813–1900), the founder of Elberon, was born in Rahway but lived in Elberon until he died. He is buried in Greenwood Cemetery in Brooklyn, New York. (Durnell Collection.)

Cornelius Vanderbilt, "The Commodore," is shown here in an 1897 photograph taken at the Elberon Hotel Cottage. (Durnell Collection.)

Walt Whitman (1819–1892) was a frequent visitor to Long Branch. This photograph was taken in Washington, D.C., during the Civil War. (Durnell Collection.)

120

Horace Greeley (1811–1872), an editor of the *New York Tribune* and a famous gold rush entrepreneur, stayed at the West End Hotel in 1860. Greeley, Colorado, is named after this famous character. (Durnell Collection.)

This portrait of Cornelius Vanderbilt (1794–1877) was made in 1860. (Durnell Collection.)

William H. Vanderbilt (1821–1885) posed for this 1875 portrait. (Durnell Collection.)

Sir Thomas Lipton (1850–1931), the famous Americas Cup skipper, is shown here in 1915. (Durnell Collection.)

Gustave W. Pach (1849–1904) took this self-portrait in 1898. The Pach Brothers were in the photography business until the 1980s. (Durnell Collection.)

This image depicts the finale of the Grant Ball at the Stetson House on July 27, 1869. (Durnell Collection.)

Bernard Baruch (1870–1965) and his brothers spent their summers at Cedar Avenue, Elberon Avenue, Ocean Avenue, and Atlantic Avenue. (Durnell Collection.)

This Pach photograph shows a group of unidentified hunters around the turn of the century. We can only assume the guns are not loaded by the way they are being handled. (Durnell Collection.)

The sign in the center of this group of hunters around the turn of the century reads "Boys Keep Out." (Durnell Collection.)

A lawn party, or possibly a wedding, is shown here in 1879. (Durnell Collection.)

Alfred J. Meyer took this photograph of the Long Branch championship football team in 1896. Long Branch still produces championship teams one hundred years later. (Long Branch Library Collection.)

This satire about Oscar Wilde appeared in *Harper's Weekly* in 1882. Thomas Nast, the author of *The Night before Christmas*, may have been the artist. (Durnell Collection.)

A young man is shown here studying "nature" through a telescope at the seashore in July 1869. (Durnell Collection.)

This satire about the stage crew at the Broadway Theater in Long Branch was signed by Bradly Martin of Martin & Fabrini. (Durnell Collection.)

Acknowledgments

First I want to thank my wife Joanne and my son Shane, for spending many hours with me hunting for the old landmarks of Long Branch. I especially want to thank the Long Branch Free Public Library for access to the James Durnell collection of photographs. Last but not least I want to thank the Public Affairs Department of Monmouth Medical Center for their help in obtaining the early photographs of Monmouth Memorial Hospital.